GLORY CARRIERS

RELEASING THE GLORY OF GOD
INTO YOUR EVERY DAY!

CHRISTOPHER FLEETCROFT

www.glorycarriers.co.uk

CONTENTS

ACKNOWLEDGMENTS

I want to thank the Revive Church family for all your support and encouragement. It's an honour to work, laugh and even cry together. May God continue to bless and grow us.

Jarrod Cooper, thank you for your leadership and encouraging me to go further. This has been an incredible adventure.

Writing a book has been much harder than I thought and none of this would have been possible without my friend, Helen Tilling. Thank you for transforming my thoughts and ideas into coherent text. You are an incredible blessing!

PREFACE

I remember, as if it was yesterday, witnessing God's Presence not only visiting but resting upon Hull over a significant period of time about ten years ago! This resulted in an incredible outpouring of His Holy Spirit, which touched and radically changed many, many lives both within and outside of the church walls!

However, my heart was broken as I subsequently observed men and women who had burned so brightly at the start, reduced to nothing more than glowing embers as life got in the way! Hence the reason for this book!

I long to see those who are hungry for God to move powerfully through their lives again, experience Him not just in a meeting, or during times of refreshing, but at all times and on every occasion!

The principles contained in this book are biblical designs, intended to help us learn how to dig out, build and maintain internal structures which will continually catch and store the Glory of God, and then encourage us to release it through natural overflow into our every day - transforming not only our lives, but those around us!

INTRODUCTION

Outpouring!

One weekend in September 2011, quite unexpectedly, the Glory of God was poured out on our church. Our senior leader, Jarrod Cooper, had invited Evangelist Nathan Morris to minster at a weekend conference. It was a conference like no other I have ever experienced in my thirty years of Christian life, the atmosphere thick with the presence of God! During that first weekend there were reports of six deaf ears being opened, lame people walking and pain leaving bodies. Monday came and church staff, overwhelmed by God's presence, lay around the office. People were sharing their faith at work and ringing the church, asking for it to be opened so they could come and pray.

As the weeks rolled by; prodigals were returning to church, more and more stories of healings and salvations were pouring in and the presence of God continued to fill our services.

GLORY CARRIERS

The Holy Spirit fell on me in a way I had only read about and it felt like I was living in a Holy Spirit bubble for three months! God was so close, real and tangible. If I listened to worship music I would often be completely caught up, worshipping Father with tears streaming down my face, and I lost the taste for probably my biggest vice – watching television! All I wanted to do was pray, read my Bible and see God's Glory invade the earth.

I was contacting everyone I knew, telling them that they needed to get to Hull; I was thinking this is it! Revival has broken out! What I had been praying and hoping for, for years, was coming true before my eyes. I remember sitting in the church office, laughing uncontrollably as I heard about the latest healing of one of our long term seriously ill congregation. Why was I laughing? We were running out of sick people!

The whole of Hull impacted by the power of God? It seemed obvious that it was only a matter of time! The Kingdom of God was rolling out across our city and it appeared unstoppable! When praying for the sick, our mindsets soon changed from hoping God would heal them, to astonishment when He didn't!

During this time I was working as a teacher in a youth club and have no idea how I was able to keep my job! Sharing the gospel was easy, but writing lesson plans and filling in spreadsheets was such an unwelcome distraction; all I wanted to do was dive back into prayer. Then one day, my boss - and good friend - came to my desk, asking why our church was advertising for a youth pastor? The news hit me like a sucker punch to my stomach, I could hardly move! I knew Holy Spirit was leading me into my next chapter; that job was mine! At the start of 2012, I joined the church staff team as youth pastor.

In March of that year we held another conference, taking over and filling the City Hall. It was incredible! People were getting out of wheelchairs and documented healings were taking place, alongside an immense sense of the Glory of God. A few weeks earlier, my senior leader had sat me down and asked if I would use the youth team to host an outreach meeting outside the City Hall. His proposal filled me with dread, but Holy Spirit prompted me to say "Yes!"

I had taken the youth onto the streets before and we had witnessed salvations and healings, but that was purely through us approaching others! The day finally arrived and I was fasting, though not from choice; I was just too nervous to eat - and I like to eat! The biggest meeting I had taken to date was in the safety of a church building with no more than fifty people in attendance. A crowd of around six hundred men, women and children were now gathered expectantly in the city centre!

As I was walking out to welcome them, my friend asked me; "How are we going to do this? Words of knowledge?" My response – "Yes!" The only problem being, I had no experience of *using* words of knowledge in a meeting, however, my ear *was* feeling a bit fuzzy! - so I figured that maybe God was trying to get my attention about hearing issues, and in front of six hundred folk in the city centre, declared that God was going to heal people and invited all those who were deaf to come forward.

Some of the team sang a worship song as others prayed for those who had stepped up, and then, to the glory of God, people who had been prayed for actually began witnessing to the rest of the crowd of how they had been healed of deafness! We then prayed for anyone else with a need who wanted to come forward, and once again, God's Spirit was poured out in the middle of the town centre with more healings taking place - including a man giving up his crutches.

I had given strict instructions on how to pray for people, making sure to keep them all upright; yet, overwhelmed by His Glory, folk had fallen where they stood and were now littering the street around the City Hall! After we had finished our meeting, team members remained in the crowd for some time, continuing to minister and witness to those in need.

On a separate occasion I accompanied the youth team onto a Hull council estate, and within a couple of hours we saw over twenty people making decisions for Christ. I watched as a couple of our teenage girls approached five young ladies coming from a block of flats. Within a few minutes they had shared the gospel, and all five had been led through the sinner's prayer! The Holy Spirit directed me across to one young lad and I shared the gospel with him, but after responding positively he promptly ran off! Twenty minutes later, he returned with one of his mates and asked me to share the gospel with him, while he disappeared once again, found another friend and brought him back so that he too could receive Jesus into his life!

A few months later I sent a team into town; within two hours they had returned, excited that over fifty people had responded to the gospel!

I Was Wrong!

In June of 2013 we held another conference in the City Hall and I was asked, once again, to hold an open air service with the help of the youth team. This time we saw the blind see, the deaf hear and the lame walk - an incredible amount of healing taking place through the simple, faith-filled prayers of the young! One older lady, who had arrived supported by a walking frame, was prayed for by two of the girls and ended up running around the crowd, with the teenagers struggling to keep up! She then ran off leaving her walker behind before we could share the gospel. A few minutes later, to our relief, she came back. I was thinking that Holy Spirit had been working on her and she would now accept Jesus. I was wrong! The lady had simply forgotten her keys, and taking them from the now redundant walking frame, she left again!

This was not a one off occurrence; we met many people who were eager to receive healing but not interested in hearing about Jesus! We led many through the sinner's prayer of repentance but only ever managed to persuade a few of them to come to church. Of those we *were* able to get through the door, most didn't make it back a second time. To my shame, I have no idea where any of the twenty-five people who made a commitment to Christ on that council estate are now. Of the countless number of people we led to Jesus on the streets, I only know of one who is still with us!

I thought an outbreak of healing and miracles, with such an awareness of God's presence, was the key to church growth. I was wrong about this too! There *were* prodigals who returned to church during this time and now live transformed, God fearing lives; however, many others have disappeared once again. Seeing people get out of wheelchairs became such a routine occurrence, that when faced with the choice of coming to church and seeing God perform miraculous works versus watching their favourite television show - television inevitably won! The church down the road is not your competition for your people's attention – the world is!

It Was the Best of Times, It Was the Worst of Times...

When I remember those days it triggers an incredible sense of awe but also a deep feeling of sadness. Many people who stood with us during this time have since left the church; many people are no longer walking with the Lord...

God poured out His Spirit and it didn't solve everything; in fact, many situations were made worse! Problems and disputes which already existed in the church body were magnified and brought to the surface. Our pastoral system broke down, our integration system broke down, our leadership broke down! The wine had been poured out, but the wineskin couldn't contain it and had broken; the wine was now wasted on the ground!

> *"And no one pours new wine into old wineskins. Otherwise, the new wine will burst the skins; the wine will run out and the wineskins will be ruined."*
> Luke 5:37 NIV

Nursemaids and Intercessors

From my study of revivals this is not uncommon. One of my favourite books is, 'Rees Howells Intercessor', by Norman Grubb. In this account of the Welsh Revival, Grubb laments about how many of those who were touched by the revival, later walked away from their faith.

> *"But the real problem arose as the Revival proceeded and thousands were added to the churches. There were more children born than there were nurses to feed them. The establishing of converts became the greatest need, which if*

*not met would be the most dangerous weakness
of the Revival."[1]*

With so many new converts, there were not enough teachers to go round who could teach them how to live. In other words; these new believers were not being discipled. The other need that Grubb highlighted is that there were not enough intercessors to pray the young converts through to fullness of faith. There are parts of Wales which were deeply impacted by the revival, that are now reported to be the hardest places to reach.

The wine was poured out and spilled on the ground!

I live for outpouring! but, I value the wine so much I cannot bear for even a single drop to be spilled; because I love the wine – I love the wineskin!

---

[1] Rees Howells Intercessor by Norman Grubb

1. THE WORD AND THE SPIRIT

In the leadership circles I frequently move in, people often sub-divide local churches, aside from their denomination, into one of two different and distinct categories; Word churches and Spirit churches. I wonder which style of church you share an affinity with?

Spirit churches love flowing in the gifts of the Holy Spirit and have an expectation of encounter within their meetings, which tend to be on the smaller side. They love to be spontaneous and planning is often a dirty word, with emphasis given on flowing with the Spirit. They will use verses like John 3:8 to justify their chaotic style of church and why it is superior and more biblical than a Word church. - *"The wind blows wherever it pleases. You hear its sound, but you cannot tell where it comes from or where it is going. So it is with everyone born of the Spirit."*[1]

In the extreme they are often weird, wacky, unorganised and chaotic; in other words, they lack structure.

---

[1] John 3:8 NIV

Word churches on the other hand, will use verses such as 1 Corinthians 14:33 to justify why *their* style of church is superior and more biblical than a Spirit church; *"For God is not a God of disorder but of peace - as in all the congregations of the Lord's people."[1]*

Word churches love order and organisation, and their emphasis is on sound doctrine, teaching and programmes. Every service and department are meticulously planned, with both stability and time-keeping highly valued! but, in the extreme they are monotonous, lifeless and dry; in other words they lack living water.

Just before he died in 1947, Smith Wigglesworth prophesied:

> *"When the new church phase is on the wane, there will be evidence in the churches of something that has not been seen before: a coming together of those with an emphasis on the Word and those with an emphasis on the Spirit.*
> *When the Word and the Spirit come together, there will be the biggest move of the Holy Spirit that the nations, and indeed, the world have ever seen. It will mark the beginning of a revival that will eclipse anything that has been witnessed*

---

[1] 1 Corinthians 14:33 NIV

within these shores, even the Wesleyan and Welsh revivals of former years.
The outpouring of God's Spirit will flow over from the United Kingdom to mainland Europe, and from there, will begin a missionary move to the ends of the earth."

We know that the church is not a building, it is the people of God. Our local churches are made up of people; some who tend toward the Word and some who tend towards the Spirit. In fact, the emphasis on the prophecy from Smith is on the *people* coming together not organisations.

In all honesty I tend towards the Spirit; I love prophecy! I want to know what God is saying now! I cringe inwardly when people ask me to teach on a specific topic with set notes and will do my best to preach on what is burning on my heart at that specific time! So, week two of a ten week discipleship course and I'm already being a bit naughty, ripping up the notes and changing things into a prophetic prayer night. It's not that I'm unfocused, more that I'm focused on how the river is flowing.

I have come to learn the value of teachers who love to teach the principles of faith and doctrine; they are so good at building people up in their faith and I need such people in my church to balance out my prophetic voice. I need leaders who are willing to walk with people building principle upon principle, so that our congregation will grow to become natural Glory containers; built according to the plans of God. I need people who are focused on structure.

Jesus commanded us to go into all the world; healing the sick, casting out demons and making disciples - teaching them everything He had already taught. We are called to move in the power of God (Spirit) and at the very same time, disciple people with His teaching (Word).

We need to value both people of the Spirit and people of the Word. We need each other! I don't want to see another outpouring of God where the wine is poured out and wasted on the ground. I love the wine, so I have learnt to love the wineskin.

I really dislike prayer times that are driven by a list of needs. In my quiet times I love to worship God, seek His face, hear what He's saying, and speak what I hear into being through prayer. However, I have come to value people who regularly pray for me and my church on a set, time-tabled basis. It's comforting to know that my life and the lives of others are diligently prayed for through structured prayer strategies, rather than my ad hoc prophetic utterances.

If the people of the Spirit and the people of the Word are to come together, we need to appreciate that we are not perfect. Our understanding of God and His ways is often filtered through what we have been taught and our own personal experience. We need to be humble enough to understand we do not know it all. God has made each of us unique, and the body comes together with different purposes and understandings.

It's time for the people of the Spirit to recognise and value the planning and structures of those who tend towards the Word; and it's time for the people of the Word to embrace the life and spontaneity that flows through the Spirit, even when understanding alludes them.

Division is often driven by fear; fear of the unknown! It's a great thing when people from different churches come together to pray, however, I have attended 'unity' meetings where the only unity in the room was in the title of the meeting!

When I went to university, I had the opportunity to meet many Christians from different church backgrounds. One of the nicest and holiest Christians I met, was a Baptist girl who had been taught that tongues were a manifestation of the devil, and prophecy was not for today!

Whenever I felt I could do with some encouragement, I would knock on the door of her dorm and be greeted by her warm and friendly face. I wouldn't have long to wait before she'd let me know that while praying for me that week, she'd had some thoughts, which she had jotted down and would then pass on to me. I still have many of them to this day and they are some of the best prophetic words I have ever received.

By not arguing over theology or terminology, I was able to encounter the Glory of God and build a friendship with someone who disagreed with me. We were able to pray together and witness together. I could see the Glory of God flowing through her life; and when I was accused by her church leaders of committing heresy, she stood by me, knowing I was completely genuine and full of God's love.

I believe that many of our church unity meetings should actually start without prayer, teaching or projects. I believe we should start by *first* eating together; by getting to know each other. Break down the walls of mistrust and get to understand each other's terminology. Words are exceptionally powerful and extremely versatile, and different people and organisations may use the same word or phrase to signify something completely the opposite! Offence is simply a by-product of misunderstanding the meaning or intention behind someone else's use of language!

I believe such an approach will actually lead to powerful prayer meetings, where leaders in a city gather with one heart and one mind - rather than a prayer meeting in name only where all the prayer is undone by mistrust.

Synergy

There is a synergy when the Word and the Spirit come together. When I look at the scriptures there seems to be no division between the two; in fact, we say that scripture is inspired by the Holy Spirit - in other words, that Holy Spirit wrote the book!

Jesus said, "My words are Spirit and Life".[1]
 -The Word contains the Spirit

The Sword of the Spirit is the Word of God.[2]
 -The Word of God is the instrument of the Spirit

Jesus said "I am the Way, the Truth, and the Life."[3]

The Spirit is the Spirit of Truth and the Spirit of Life, and we are supposed to walk in step with the Spirit.

Through my study of the scriptures and my experiences of witnessing God moving in power and healing, I believe there is a great synergy of Spirit and Word coming together, rather than being separated. I believe we need to change our understanding of the concept of the Spirit and the Word. When we encounter God, we encounter Him in Spirit and in Truth - to reject one is to reject both; to accept one is to accept both; to experience one is to experience both!

---

[1] John 6:63
[2] Ephesians 6:17
[3] John 14:6

Reflection
- Have I become so reliant on my routines that God's power is only an optional extra?
- Is there somebody I should be reaching out to across a theological divide?

2. THE GREAT EVIL

*"My people have committed two sins: They have
forsaken me, the spring of living water, and
have dug their own cisterns, broken cisterns that
cannot hold water."*
Jeremiah 2:13 NIV

In the book of Jeremiah, God uses His prophet Jeremiah to deliver a dire warning to His people of impending judgement and exile to Babylon, because of their wickedness. God summarises their evil in two sins:

1. Forsaking God who is the spring of living water.
If we reject the Holy Spirit, the Living Water – we reject God!
Jesus talks about there being only one unforgivable sin; blasphemy of the Holy Spirit! What is the context of Matthew 12 where Jesus talks about this unforgiveable sin? The Pharisees were attributing the works of the Spirit of God, to demons! Be careful about judging manifestations of the Spirit.

2. Creating man-made broken structures that cannot hold (living) water.

A cistern is a structure that stores water so it can be used when needed, and those talked about in Jeremiah were built specifically to collect rainwater. Unfortunately, in this passage the people have built the cisterns to their own design and they are broken and completely useless.

To be in the Will of God for our lives, we need to embrace the Spirit and build structures according to His design that are able to catch the rain.

Many believers love the tangible presence of God within our church meetings. They bathe under the waterfall of the Holy Spirit through worship and ministry and feel clean, energised and refreshed; then comes Monday morning and there's that irritating person in the office, or an argument at home, or the bills that can't be payed! Sunday morning suddenly seems so far away, and although they wish they could be back there under the waterfall of His presence, that experience is now long gone and completely unrelatable to their everyday life.

What's happening here? These people know how to *experience* the Holy Spirit, but don't know how to *carry* the Holy Spirit with them. When we position ourselves under the waterfall, we need to go with a bucket and take the water with us when we leave. We are called to be Glory carriers; not just people who experience the Glory of God but those who carry and release the Glory of God!

THE GREAT EVIL

Jesus said that we are the light of the world - we are supposed to bring life and light into every environment!

How do we do it? We fill our bucket from the waterfall and carry it with us throughout the following week! Then, on Monday morning when we get to the office and that irritating colleague annoys us, we take a cup, fill it up from our bucket and have a drink - then we offer them a drink too; and when your friend shares that they are contemplating suicide, you give them a drink from your bucket; and when you meet someone who needs healing, you pray for them! In other words, you give them a drink from your bucket.

A common cistern in most western houses is the toilet. Above the bowl of the toilet is a tank of water, and when the toilet is flushed, water rushes down from the cistern into the bowl and you can then hear the tank refilling from your water supply until it holds enough water for its next flush.

When I was newly married and moved into our home, the silence of each night would regularly be interrupted by a 'pssst' sound coming from the bathroom several times an hour! Putting on my new 'man of the house' mantle, I quickly traced the sound to the toilet and consequently decided I needed to solve this irritating quirk! Not really knowing what I was doing I took the toilet apart on the bathroom floor; and, after buying replacement parts that didn't fit, replacing parts that probably didn't need replacing and buying tools I would never use again, finally discovered that the toilet had a faulty seal in the cistern and therefore water was constantly leaking into the bowl! When the water in the cistern dropped to a certain level, a valve would open to fill the cistern back up again. The 'pssst' sound I could hear was the water flowing through the pipes and topping up the water level, thus enabling the toilet to flush on demand.

This led me to thinking! Wouldn't it be great if we were also in constant connection with God when we were in the office; continually being filled up with him? The sound of Heaven downloading into your office and causing the Glory of God to overflow into the environment around you! I'm sure for some of you, your work colleagues already experience and may even talk about, a change in the atmosphere when you're around; as if light and love flood the space that you reside in.

Let the living water of Heaven flow through you, bringing eternal life to those around you.

To be Glory carriers, we need to love the Holy Spirit and partner with Him to build structures that will catch and store the life giving Holy Spirit within us. We need to learn about God's systems and structures as He sets them in place within our lives, so that through them, we will be able to store the fullness of life and release it as needed. To love the Holy Spirit is to love these pathways.

Reflection
When was the last time you were filled with the Holy Spirit? Have you ever been filled with the Holy Spirit? Why not ask Him to fill you now? Take a few minutes to close your eyes, relax and ask Holy Spirit to fill you.

3. LEARN TO CATCH THE RAIN

Jesus approaches an outcast Samaritan woman and shares an amazing verse about being Glory carriers;

> *"Everyone who drinks this water will be thirsty again, but whoever drinks the water I give them will never thirst. Indeed, the water I give them will become in them a spring of water welling up to eternal life."*
> John 4:13-14 NIV

His promise is that those who follow him will be filled with the living water of the Holy Spirit! Their conversation progresses to worship and she complains that even though the Samaritans have their own place of worship on the mountain, the Jews insist they must travel to Jerusalem; can she not worship God nearer to home? Jesus replies that soon the physical location to worshipping God will not be an issue, and then declares:

*"But the time is coming--indeed it's here now--
when true worshippers will worship the Father in
spirit and in truth. The Father is looking for those
who will worship him that way."*
John 4:23 NIV

After promising that the water He gives would become a spring of living water welling up within us to eternal life; Jesus explains that as believers, we will now be able to worship God in a new way! No longer do we need to go to the temple to meet with God. No longer do we need to go to a church service to encounter the waterfall from Heaven. Whenever we choose to, and wherever we are, we can turn our hearts towards our Saviour and go directly into the throne room of God.

*"Let us then approach God's throne of grace
with confidence, so that we may receive mercy
and find grace to help us in our time of need."*
Hebrews 4:16 NIV

I often share with those whose lives I speak into, that it's my hope they will have greater experiences with God in their personal devotional times than they do within their church services! The Apostle Paul advises us to be continually filled with the Holy Spirit at all times and on all occasions. You do not need to wait for the next conference or the next service; God is wanting to fill you right now! Your birth-right as a child of God is open access to the throne room of God; in fact, it's expected!

I love leading meetings with a select few people who know how to pray and seek God for themselves. As a meeting host, it's like throwing a lit match into a petrol-soaked pile of wood! As a worship leader, duff notes are irrelevant as whichever song you choose will take off and fly. If you stop, the room will carry on without you. Leadership becomes about gently pulling on the rudder of a ship, not trying to push start a car!

Jesus teaches us that when we pray we are to get on our own, shut the door and the Father will meet with us.[1]

Intentional Connection

I intentionally put time aside for my wife and family; it's only logical that I also intentionally put time aside to connect with God and the best time for me to do this is first thing in the morning. I find that following a time of prayer, I'm a better, more energy-filled and loving person for the remainder of the day. Furthermore, I'm also more likely to spontaneously encounter God during the day if I've intentionally met with Him in the morning – rather than if I haven't!

I have also discovered that if I'm feeling dry and disconnected, it's very easy to busy myself doing good things and use these as an

---

[1] Matthew 6:6

excuse, instead of slowing down and being intimate with my Father in prayer.

A few months before I got married, the vision of my wedding day pushed me into an exercise schedule early in the morning and at 6pm each evening. Once married however, that schedule was for the birds alone; dinner was now served at 6pm, and I could no longer disappear early in the morning before work! I had to adapt and come up with a new exercise schedule, so I did! I got that schedule up and running and it was working well....and then we had a baby! Once again I had to rearrange my life, but I managed - by going for an early run and then showering at the office! It took organisation but it worked!

At one point in my life I would wake at 4:30am every day and spend time in prayer before the rest of the household woke up. When I try that now I'm grumpy and tired! My life has changed and I have had to adapt my prayer schedule accordingly. I've become very creative in making late nights and family time work together. Currently, walking the dog forms part of my prayer life strategy - as do coffee shop visits where I'll sit with my headphones plugged in! These are just two of the prayer routines I have built into my day; another is to get my guitar out at home and blast the neighbours!

My advice is; if *you* have something that works, build on it. Too many times I have heard about someone's amazing prayer life and tried to copy their schedule, only to wreck my own personal prayer routine in the process! We are all different! just try to make sure that you read God's Word, spend some time in reflection and actually pray each day, but don't let people change something that is already working for you!

Reflection

- What routines have you built into your schedule to catch the rain?
- Are there any structural changes to your life that you are considering to increase your capacity?

4. FOUNDATIONS FOR GLORY

'On the last and greatest day of the festival,
Jesus stood and said in a loud voice, "Let anyone
who is thirsty come to me and drink. Whoever
believes in me, as Scripture has said, rivers of
living water will flow from within them." By this
he meant the Spirit...'
John 7:33-39 NASB

I read this passage a while ago and had a bit of an argument with God.

"Come on God...this doesn't happen...!!!"

I witness many people genuinely receiving the Holy Spirit; definitely not faking it! I can clearly see the Holy Spirit all over them and yet their lives are not transformed. They come back the following week just as broken, just as dry. The Holy Spirit has been poured out and yet it doesn't seem to be working - either the Bible is true or it's not!

So I studied and meditated on this verse. The first explanation I considered, was that the verse says "many rivers" - maybe they just weren't experiencing the *right* river? However, my understanding of Paul's instructions about the Holy Spirit to the church at Corinth quickly shut down that avenue of thought.

My second train of thought was that the verse can be understood to mean; to drink and keep on drinking! However, the context of the Samaritan woman just doesn't stack up as a good enough explanation for me.

Finally, after a few days of wrestling with this Bible verse I asked Holy Spirit and immediately got the following phrase as a thought; "They come to wash but they do not drink."

When you bathe, you wash off the sweat and dirt and become clean and refreshed on the outside. When you drink, water enters into your body and becomes part of you, transforming the makeup of your body from the inside.

When you drink of the Holy Spirit, you are allowing God to transform you from the inside out! The people who come only to *wash* in the waterfall of Heaven will most certainly be refreshed, and even cleansed, believing that their lives have been changed; but, this will only ever be at surface level and the effects short-lived! They are not allowing the Holy Spirit to get inside of them and transform their behaviours or mindsets on a deeper level, which would then result in longer lasting, if not permanent, change. People who bathe are experiencing the power of the Holy Spirit but are not allowing the experience to shape them. In other words; they choose not to obey or follow the Holy Spirit's guidance!

Jesus told a story about two builders; one who built his house on the sand and one who built his house on a rock. Both builders heard God speak – or, both went to church, read their Bibles and listened to God's instruction. The builder who built on the rock chose to follow what God said; whereas the builder whose life ended in chaos, listened but chose not to obey!

If we want to be a vessel containing the Glory of God, a vessel that holds the water of eternal life, we need to obey God. We need to take hold of, and build on, the structures of Godly living as set out in the Bible; following the leading of the Holy Spirit in every area of our lives. Jesus said that those who believe in Him drink of the water; those who believe in Him put into practice what He says.

We need to allow the sword of the Spirit to carve foundations from our innermost being, so that we can contain His Glory.

The Apostle Paul writes; "...we instructed you how to live in order to please God,"[1] before setting down rules for holy living. This is post-cross, grace-filled teaching by Paul. He audaciously states that if you reject the structures for holy living he has given, you are not rejecting him, you are rejecting; "God who gives you His Holy Spirit to you."[2]

---

[1] 1 Thessalonians 4:1 NIV
[2] 1 Thessalonians 4:8 NASB

If you reject New Testament biblical morality, you are rejecting the river of God. You may be able to splash around in the water quite happily but you will not have the ability to store. Someone who confesses to love God but then follows their own desires and passions, is nothing more than a broken cistern that cannot hold water.

I meet people who claim to be Glory carriers and watch as they run from one revival meeting to another, yet their lives remain untransformed and are ineffective in their witness. They may come back from the latest outpouring soaking wet, but unless they allow God to transform them from the inside out, they are Glory experiencers and not Glory carriers.

> *"...what counts is whether we really have been changed into new and different people."*
> Galatians 6:15 TLB

I remember the most powerful encounter I had with the Holy Spirit; I woke up the next morning in a bubble of Heaven's Glory - it was immense! When I arrived at work, I found myself getting carried away sharing all that had happened during the conference I'd attended the previous weekend, but even though I knew I was going to be late for an appointment, I still wanted a coffee! I dashed into the kitchen and in my hurry, decided to completely disregard all the new coffee-making rules that my boss had expressly laid out. This may not seem like the crime of the century, but I was shocked to realise that even though I was experiencing the tangible presence of Heaven, I was still able to be dishonest and do something I knew was wrong.

There are many stories in the Bible where the anointed of God sin. Being in the river does *not* mean you have lost the ability to sin!

I continued to experience being caught up in a bubble of God's presence 24/7 throughout the next few months. During this time, I decided to make some changes to cultivate a lifestyle of His Glory. I started reading daily devotionals and other Christian books, stopped watching certain television programmes and intentionally freed up time to study the Bible. The choices I made in those months set me up for the next few years of healings and miracles in church ministry. What was I doing? I was building structures - cisterns - in my life, to catch the water of life.

When you build structures following His designs not yours, those structures will sustain you from a wet season through a dry one.

Reflection
- Are there any habits God is putting His finger on that you need to sort?
- Have you turned a deaf ear towards God's prompting in the past and no longer follow His direction in a certain area?

5. HEARING THE VOICE

One of my favourite passages in the Bible is found in Hebrews, where the writer quotes Jeremiah:

> *"The days are coming, declares the Lord,*
> *when I will make a new covenant*
> *with the people of Israel*
> *and with the people of Judah.*
> *⁹ It will not be like the covenant*
> *I made with their ancestors*
> *when I took them by the hand*
> *to lead them out of Egypt,*
> *because they did not remain faithful to my covenant,*
> *and I turned away from them,*
> *declares the Lord.*
> *¹⁰ This is the covenant I will establish with the people of Israel*
> *after that time, declares the Lord.*
> *I will put my laws in their minds*
> *and write them on their hearts.*
> *I will be their God,*
> *and they will be my people.*

> [11] *No longer will they teach their neighbor,*
> *or say to one another, 'Know the Lord,'*
> *because they will all know me,*
> *from the least of them to the greatest.*
> [12] *For I will forgive their wickedness*
> *and will remember their sins no more."*
> Hebrews 8:8-12 NIV

A few years ago I was in the Czech Republic attending an incredible youth conference. One of the events scheduled into the weekend programme was an afternoon of outreach, and so I, along with nearly one hundred passionate young people, descended on a nearby small town eager to share the gospel! There were only a handful of local residents out on the streets and they were completely overwhelmed by the vast amount of visitors wanting to share Jesus with them.

I found myself walking through the park with two young women who were very keen to find someone to witness to and, thankfully, were able to speak both English and Czech! One of them pointed out a lady sitting with her daughter on a bench and felt prompted that we should minister to them.

Whenever I take part in street ministry, I'm longing for people to simply encounter God rather than try to win arguments or recite prayers of confession. It soon became apparent, however, that the lady we had approached was after an entirely different encounter - an encounter with my wallet! Every thread of our conversation led us back to her saying that she needed money! I decided we were just wasting our time and so, hoping to make a quick exit, did what I usually do and asked if she wanted prayer for anything! Well she did want prayer and you've guessed it - she needed money!

So I prayed that this lady would have her needs met, and was just about to leave when the Holy Spirit reminded me that praying for someone in need and not helping them when you are able to, makes your prayer useless![1] In my mind I began to argue with the Lord; "But Father, she's been trying to manipulate me from the very beginning.....!"
Then memories of Danny Silk[2] - teaching about taking responsibility for your own actions, and not allowing other people's behaviour to change the way you respond to them – flashed across my mind.

Holy Spirit then asked me; "Do you believe she needs money?"
"Well....yes!" I replied.
"Do you have the means to help?"
"Yes....!"

Reluctantly I pulled out my wallet, and taking out about twenty pounds handed it to the woman. In that instant it was like Heaven had opened! The woman was crying, the young lady interpreting for me was crying, and well...so was I! It's amazing what can happen when you follow the voice of God in simple obedience. My interpreter was then able to really minister to the lady, while I

---

[1] James 2:15-17
[2] Danny Silk, senior leader of Bethel church in Redding, California

looked around to see where the other young woman who had travelled into town with us had got to!

She was busy witnessing to the young daughter, who was probably around six years old, on a nearby bench. I wasn't very comfortable with this as I believed the girl was too young to be witnessed to without her mum, so went over to put an end to it. I got within a couple of steps of them and suddenly encountered the most sweet, heavenly fragrance! I say fragrance, but it was more like smelling with my eyes! Instead of stopping what was going on, I turned to look at the girls mother and somehow, through the use of sign language, I was able to understand that she was giving me permission to talk to her daughter.

I asked the girl to stretch out her hand, and then prayed that the Holy Spirit would fill her hand with His presence without me touching her! This was translated across by the interpreter, and the young girl's face lit up in wonder as she exclaimed she could feel something. Well, we carried on until she announced that she could feel this warm, indescribable sensation throughout her entire body! At this point, I stepped out in faith a little further and prayed; "Lord, let her hear your voice!" Before the young woman could translate what I had prayed, the child started babbling excitedly in Czech! I turned to the interpreter, as the only word I know in Czech is thank you, only to see her jaw drop in amazement.

"What's happening?" I asked.

"She says she can hear God talking to her!", the stunned young lady replied.

Please remember, the young girl had not yet had my prayer translated to her! I was also shocked! I know I'd prayed that prayer but I hadn't meant literally!! I think I'd hoped that she would experience some kind of 'a sense' that God was real, but to be honest I don't really know what I'd meant! Myself and my interpreter were no longer needed, as the young girl chatted happily to Jesus without us!

That event reminded me of the prophecy given through Jeremiah; that no longer would people need a teacher because they would hear from the Lord for themselves. The New Covenant means that God now speaks directly to His people.

Hearts and Minds

Many churches create a new covenant by adapting the old one! Laws relating to temple requirements and other cultural matters may be removed; such as rules for business, or the preparation of food! Others may simply be up-dated - changing the giving of a tithe from the temple to the local church, for example, or how to look after visitors. New laws will undoubtedly be added; reading the Bible, attending church, not smoking.....but this is not the New Covenant!

You will not find the New Covenant written in your church mission statement or hidden on your bookshelf. God did not write the New Covenant on stone, paper or computer screens, but on something infinitely more precious; the hearts and minds of His people.

The New Covenant in no way resembles the Old! It isn't a written list of rules we try hard to interpret and obey through reasoning. If the Old Covenant was a letter from Heaven; the New Covenant is more like a smart phone, where we have the opportunity to not just send and receive texts but enjoy video calls with our Heavenly Father! However, even that analogy doesn't go far enough! The New Covenant transforms people into the very likeness of God[1]; who think like Him, act like Him, talk like Him, heal like Him, are Holy like Him.

The Original Plan

To understand the New Covenant, it's worth taking a pause to re-examine the original covenant plan. God declares to the people of Israel, through Moses, that they will be His people if they do two things: obey His voice and keep His Covenant[2]. It is God's plan that the whole nation of Israel will be priests,[3] not just the tribe of Levi.

Under instruction from the Lord, the whole nation consecrated themselves and gathered at the foot of Mount Sinai where God descended as fire.[4] Thick, billowing smoke consumed the whole mountain and it shook violently; and when Moses spoke with God, God replied in the thunder and lightning! The Bible states that the Israelites physically saw the thunder, so could it be that they

---

[1] 2 Corinthians 3:18
[2] Exodus 19:5
[3] Exodus 19:6
[4] Exodus 19:18

witnessed the actual words of God as He delivered the Ten Commandments to His people?

The Israelites complained that hearing God's voice was too terrifying for them! They pleaded with Moses to speak with God on their behalf and then let them know what He'd said? God agreed to their request; so Moses trekked back up the mountain to speak further with God and collect the law. But, notice! this had never been the original plan! God's intention was to speak directly to His people!

As time passed and Moses still hadn't returned from the mountain, the Israelites grew impatient and began to rebel. They demanded that Aaron make gods for them, something they could worship; so collecting up their gold jewellery, Aaron cast a golden calf! When Moses finally arrived back at camp, he was incensed with rage at the behaviour of his people and threw the stone tablets, containing the Ten Commandments, to the ground where they smashed to pieces! He then issued an ultimatum; those of the Israelites who were still willing to follow the Lord were to come and stand with him. Only the tribe of Levi made their way forward! Moses then ordered them to go throughout the camp with their swords and slaughter those who had turned away - including friends, brothers and neighbours - and around three thousand people died that day! This was the turning point; the pivotal moment, when the priesthood was revoked from the nation of Israel and transferred exclusively to the members of the tribe of Levi.

One of the most important festivals in the Jewish calendar is Shavuot. Originally a harvest festival, it now also celebrates and remembers when God gave the Law (or the Torah) to the Israelites on Mount Sinai. It's usual to stay up all night learning the Torah, and then men, women and children will visit the synagogue to listen to the reading of scripture, including the Ten Commandments. Special foods are eaten during this holiday, and many Jewish people will also make pilgrimage to Jerusalem. Shavuot is also known as the 'Feast of Weeks', as this event took place seven weeks after Passover. When this feast was translated into Greek, however, instead of seven weeks it was recorded as fifty days – Pentecost!

It's no coincidence that the Holy Spirit was poured out on this day at the 'Feast of Pentecost'. In the Christian tradition, this event signifies the birth of the early church. When we sing the lines of that famous hymn, 'Send the Fire', asking for another Pentecost – for God to 'send the fire again' - we mean another outpouring; but Pentecost is so much greater than that! When the Holy Spirit was poured out, it wasn't simply an increase of power! As Peter prophesied in Acts 2, it marked the beginning of God speaking to the whole of mankind through dreams, visions and prophecy; a new age, where God would speak directly to each person through the Holy Spirit, so that they would no longer be dependent on teachers! Those who listened to Peter's message and accepted what he said, numbered around three thousand! They were all baptized and added to the church that day! This is a beautiful illustration of Word and Spirit combined.

HEARING THE VOICE

Jesus said; "My sheep hear My voice, and I know them, and they follow Me;"[1] I want to encourage you - if you've responded to the gospel, you've heard the voice of God! He doesn't always use words; sometimes He'll speak with pictures, sometimes through emotions and sometimes you'll just have 'a knowing'! God is always speaking! Our issue is one of discernment, and taking the time to tune in!

Activity

Grab your Bible, a pen and some paper, and read through the first twelve verses of the book of Ephesians, being careful to meditate on the words! Now, write down what you believe God is saying *to you* through each verse – not what you think the verse means!

Reflection

- Explain what your experience of salvation was; what made you respond?
- Have you heard the voice of God before? Describe what it sounded and felt like.
- Share what you wrote in the Ephesians activity above.

---

[1] John 10:27 NASB

6. WHAT RULES SHOULD I LIVE BY?

Simply put - we need to follow the voice of God in all areas of our lives and resist the voice of our flesh.

What is the voice of our flesh? Often when I go to the office, I'll put my gym gear in the boot of my car so I can pop to the gym for a workout on the way home. At the end of the day, however, when I find myself enjoying a burger in a fast food restaurant rather than pounding the treadmill, I know I've followed the voice of my flesh! Although I may enjoy that burger experience in the short term; in the long run once I get home, I know I would have been much happier and more at peace if I'd gone to the gym.

"The acts of the flesh are obvious: sexual immorality, impurity and debauchery; idolatry and witchcraft; hatred, discord, jealousy, fits of rage, selfish ambition, dissensions, factions and envy; drunkenness, orgies, and the like. I warn

WHAT RULES SHOULD I LIVE BY?

you, as I did before, that those who live like this
will not inherit the kingdom of God.
But the fruit of the Spirit is love, joy, peace,
forbearance, kindness, goodness, faithfulness,
gentleness and self-control. Against such things
there is no law."
Galatians 5:19-23 NIV

I find passages like this scary and, to be honest, at first glance unhelpful! Not only do I understand how easy it can be to commit acts of the flesh, I also know that many of these sinful activities are fun - that's why we do them! However, you will notice that 'joy is only mentioned in the holy part, as being a fruit of the Spirit! Furthermore, the 'don't do' list is very clear, whilst the 'do' list just seems to be a vague inventory that any eccentric do-gooder could have come up with! - don't gossip, do love, don't get drunk, be kind to one another......!

I believe the key to understanding this passage is to realise that Paul is not comparing like with like; he compares acts of the flesh with the fruit of the Spirit, rather than fruits of the Spirit with fruits of the flesh. A bit further on in the text, Paul writes; "Whoever sows to please their flesh, from the flesh will reap destruction; whoever sows to please the Spirit, from the Spirit will reap eternal life."

For instance; getting drunk (act of the flesh) can be a lot of fun and very satisfying at the time, however, the resulting drunkenness can include hangovers, weight gain, health issues, loss of memories, fights and arguments (fruit of the flesh)! Gossip may feel good and cause a bonding of people in the moment, but the fruit of gossip will eventually cause pain, distrust and a breaking down of friendships.

So what is the work of the Spirit? Unfortunately there's no set list, simply this; whatever Holy Spirit asks you to do, do it! This goes a lot further than just living right morally and following New Testament principles. Holy Spirit may ask you to go and talk to someone, serve someone, travel somewhere, even wear something specific which may seem a little weird! the list is endless! And, what is the result of following the leadings of Holy Spirit? Life! A life full of love, joy, peace, patience, kindness, goodness, faithfulness, gentleness and self-control.

> *"As for you, the anointing you received from him*
> *remains in you, and you do not need anyone to*
> *teach you. But as his anointing teaches you*
> *about all things and as that anointing is real, not*
> *counterfeit--just as it has taught you, remain in*
> *him."*
> 1 John 2:27 NIV

The above passage from the Apostle John is often skipped over by teachers and traditionalists, but if we want to live in the fullness of what Jesus bought for us at the cross, we need to learn to hear the voice of Holy Spirit and follow what He asks us to do. In fact, for

Jesus to be Lord of our lives it's imperative that we learn to. It's time to take the 'L' plates off...!!

For many years we have said that Christianity is not a set of rules but a relationship. It's time for the church to live that statement! We need God to be our best friend, lover and counsel. We need to really know Him for ourselves, not just read about Him or develop some kind of second-hand relationship through listening to others talk about Him. We need to experience God in a deep, intimate and personal way, and then the fullness of God will be revealed in the people of His body, the Church.

I can't think of a better way of summing this up than with the Bible itself. The following verse comes from one of my favourite passages; but allow the beauty and simplicity of the Passion translation to persuade you of the need for Jesus to be Lord of your life, and to follow His directions:

> *"Trust in the Lord completely, and do not rely on*
> *your own opinions.*
> *With all your heart rely on him to guide you, and*
> *he will lead you in every decision you make.*
> *Become intimate with him in whatever you do,*
> *and he will lead you wherever you go."*
> Proverbs 3:5-6 TPT

Reflection

When was the last time the Holy Spirit asked you to do something outside of your comfort zone? Did you do it?

7. GET TO THE SOURCE

During my teenage years, much fuss was made about the importance of getting into the 'River of Life' we read about in the books of Ezekiel and Revelation; bringing healing to the nations and dead places back to life. "How do I get into the River?" Or perhaps a better question; "How do I get the River of Life flowing through and out of me?" What's the secret? What's the source?

"Then the angel showed me the river of the
water of life, as clear as crystal, flowing from the
throne of God and of the Lamb"
Revelation 22:1 NIV

The source of God's power, blessing and healing in your life is God's Throne. The extent to which you allow God, Lordship *in* your life, will be the extent to which His blessing flows *through* your life! If Jesus is Lord of your finances, a river of blessing will flow through your money blessing you and the world around you. If Jesus is Lord of your relationships, healing and salvation will flow through them. When your life is completely under His Lordship, God will not only transform you, but through you, He will also transform your family, your street and even your city!

Sand is made up of fine rock and mineral particles, and so is in essence, extremely small pieces of rock. When we listen to the teachings of Jesus and weigh up each command deciding whether or not to apply it to our lives, we are building a foundation for our lives based solely on grains of truth – sand! If we follow a pick and mix Christianity, only accepting the teachings we want to, *we* are still the lord of our lives; foolish builders whose houses, built on sand with no foundations, will ultimately fall! It's only when we accept God's direction completely, that He truly becomes Lord of our lives.

Often when Christians come to me for help, they want me to listen to their problems, tell them they are justified in the decisions they have made under the circumstances and then wave my 'magic wand' of prayer, or use my position, to make their problems go away! Questions like; "What has God said to you about this?" are often unwanted and instantly dismissed. Many people will ring their pastor before seriously taking to prayer and fasting, or building a foundation of biblical morality into their life!

How often do we make plans and *then* ask God to bless them as though He's a good luck charm, rather than first taking the time to find out what *He* wants?

When I first started working for the church, my salary was reduced by a third. As a family of five, we had struggled to make ends meet with the money that had previously been coming into the house! but, knowing that God was leading us, we chose to obey. That first year in ministry was incredible; on less money we not only survived, but thrived! The only time we didn't have enough was at Christmas. We'd been very organised and managed to get presents for our children but, as December loomed, we had no money to spend on food and all the other trimmings. Yes, we could dive into using our credit cards but that seemed irresponsible other than for our basic needs.

As I was contemplating on what our family would now be thinking about our decision to journey under God's direction, and feeling pretty inadequate as a dad, one Friday evening one of my youth group gave me an envelope - and you've guessed it, there was money inside! I went home and with my wife opened the envelope stuffed with notes, and as we counted what amounted to a few hundred pounds, the excitement and enjoyment in the room was intense! I have watched movies where you see people throwing cash about like confetti and that would not be far off the scene in our living room! I wanted to go out right there and then and buy a turkey at 11 o'clock at night!! Wiser heads prevailed however, and I waited until the next morning before dashing out to do the Christmas shop.

The one time we were short during that whole year was the only time we were given a gift! When we trusted God as our provider and acknowledged Him as Lord of our finances, He moved in blessing!

Reflection

- Is Jesus Lord of your money?
- How much do you give into the ministry of the church?
- How much do you give of your surplus to those in need?

8. MEDITATION'S WHAT YOU NEED...

*"Keep this Book of the Law always on your lips;
meditate on it day and night, so that you may be
careful to do everything written in it. Then you
will be prosperous and successful."*
Joshua 1:8 NIV

If I could choose between being Joshua and Moses, I would choose Joshua. Joshua got to experience the manifest presence of God alongside Moses in the tent of meeting, however, when Moses went back to the camp, Joshua's duties would require him to remain in the tent of meeting - alone with the Glory of God! Joshua had numerous encounters with angels and experienced the voice of God speaking directly to him and passing on instruction. Yet one of the first instructions he hears is to meditate on scripture!

Some Christians believe that if you can hear the voice of God you no longer need to read the Bible. I cannot agree! Before God gave the Israelites the ten commandments, He said that to be a follower of God you needed to hear His voice and keep His commandments.

MEDITATION'S WHAT YOU NEED

God wants us to listen to what He is saying now, but also, to abide in and treasure what He has already said.

I believe the most intimate place is between your ears where your thoughts dwell; the place where our real opinions and beliefs exist and no one else comes into. What do you fill that place with - or what are your thoughts about? The plot line to your current box set? The good-looking girl who is sitting three rows in front of you? What you would spend your money on if you won the lottery?

Let me remind you about how our world is structured; you reproduce what you are intimate with! Whatever your thoughts dwell on will grow, shaping and transforming your character. That's why the Bible teaches us to meditate on the Word of God day and night. The book of Ephesians talks about the Word of God being a cleaning agent.

As you dwell on scripture and the prophecies God has given you, your thinking is purified, your desires are refined. When you start to put the Word of God on your lips, your whole body is strengthened and your environment cleansed. Meditation and confession of God's Word transforms your capacity to be a Glory carrier.

I am a great believer in listening to the voice of God and not relying solely on scripture, but here is one of my secrets to hearing His voice; God talks to me the most when I spend time in my Bible!

The Greatest Battlefield

Have you ever been in an argument or a situation that has really riled you up? Did you come away thinking; "If only I had said this", or "If only I had done that!" Did you replay the situation over and over again in your mind and every waking moment after? If this is currently something you are going through, you're dwelling on it; or let me put it in spiritual language, you are meditating on it.

When a situation arises that affects you like this, usually the next step would be to talk it over with a friend. When you explain to your friend how unfairly you've been treated, they will hopefully, on hearing your side of the story, agree with your analysis; in fact, you will be expecting them to! This process and the resulting feeling of self vindication feels good for a while, but then the negative thoughts return and you find yourself sharing with another person, and then another, desperately trying to get that sense of self vindication back again!

What's happening? You're meditating and confessing upon an offence! Before too long it's consuming your whole life; transforming your emotions, your actions and your decisions.

The person who is the 'guilty party' may be completely oblivious to the situation that's caused you pain, however, they have started to sense a negative vibe directed at them when you're around and so begin to make choices that will distance themselves from you; but this only serves to feed your sense of offence and the whole thing snowballs out of control!

50

MEDITATION'S WHAT YOU NEED

This is a massive problem in the church! Everyone has an opinion on how other people should behave, applying it especially to leaders! The reality is, we are all broken people who are made whole only through the power of God.

In second Corinthians, Paul writes a letter in response to a church situation that many of us would recognise today. Some self-appointed leaders were challenging Paul's authority and personal integrity, taking offence at the way he was running the church. They accused Paul of not being a genuine apostle and for pocketing money the church was sending to poor believers in Jerusalem.

The internet is full of accusations against Christian ministers, claiming they are immorally profiting from churches whilst also operating outside of any recognised and lawful authority. Although some mighty warriors of God have genuinely fallen into temptation, and there are undoubtedly some appalling conmen purely out to deceive, most of the accusations come from self-appointed 'watchmen' who make many false and incredibly damaging allegations!

Paul writes:

> *"For though we live in the world, we do not wage war as the world does. The weapons we fight with are not the weapons of the world. On the contrary, they have divine power to demolish strongholds. We demolish arguments*

and every pretension that sets itself up against
the knowledge of God, and we take captive
every thought to make it obedient to Christ."
2 Corinthians 10:3-5 NIV

Don't let your imagination and your speculation run away with you; take every thought captive! Don't allow offence to breed - kill it! Remember to forgive as you have been forgiven. How many times do we forgive?.....unending! I'm not saying to place yourself in a situation where you can be harmed or abused; I'm also not saying you shouldn't confront someone who has caused you offence! I am simply saying, do not let an offence consume your thought life.

How do I overcome this all consuming injustice? This is what has helped me:
Forgive them! Every time it comes up, forgive.
Speak to them; let them know you've been hurt.
Put some worship music on.
Read your Bible – but be careful with this one! Don't read the Bible through the lens of your offence; you'll find many verses you think 'the offender' needs to know, or that appear to vindicate you! Don't allow offence into you; it may initiate a greater sin in the eyes of the Father.

Let me finish with the Apostle Paul:

"Finally, brothers and sisters, whatever is true,
whatever is noble, whatever is right, whatever is
pure, whatever is lovely, whatever is

admirable—if anything is excellent or praiseworthy—think about such things."
Philippians 4:8 NIV

Activity
Go back through journals or past prophetic words and spend some time letting your imagination dwell on what you've read.

Reflection
Is there anyone you're connected to whose mistakes or failures cause you to secretly rejoice?

9. WALKING THROUGH
THE DESERT

One of my favourite passages in scripture is the infamous Psalm 23. It begins by painting a picture of Jesus the shepherd, leading his sheep – his people - into a life of rest beside pools of refreshing water. I often visualise a good personal prayer time as an oasis in the desert of this busy, secular world.

The psalmist then writes about walking 'in righteous paths' for the Glory of the Lord. I believe that as we spend time in the presence of the Lord, through prayer and scripture, righteous living should be the fruit we naturally see cultivated! As we drink of the Holy Spirit, it should so transform our behaviour that we can't help but carry His Glory into a dry and thirsty world.

So, continuing the narrative of the Psalm; we experience times of refreshing, with the Glory of God being revealed as we follow our shepherd along the paths of righteousness, but where do these paths lead? The valley of death! Surely not! That's not the gospel that was preached to me!

Too often I hear a gospel being preached today which promises that if you say 'Yes' to Jesus, everything in life will be fine; but that is *not* what Jesus promised!

> *"I have told you all this so that you may have peace in me. Here on earth you will have many trials and sorrows. But take heart, because I have overcome the world."*
> John 16:33 NLT

Jesus never said it would be easy! He promised trials, persecution and family strife to those who followed him. It's very easy when we are going through a dark time to think that somewhere along the line we must have taken a wrong turning, that we must be out of the 'Will of God'! Jesus told us to pick up our cross and follow him. Following Jesus means that we *will* take journeys through dark valleys!

I once heard a story about an old man who grew such incredible, fruit laden orange trees, they were the envy of all his neighbouring farmers. Whilst every other orange tree in the region would wilt in the hot seasons, without exception, his alone would flourish! One day, a fellow orange tree grower asked the old man what his secret was. The old man explained that when his trees were young, unlike the other farmers, he would water them sparingly. This caused the growing trees to develop deep root systems as they sought out their own underground pockets of water, then, when the hot seasons came they had access to a supply of water that trees with shallower root growth did not!

> *"Let your roots grow down into him and draw up nourishment from him. See that you go on growing in the Lord, and become strong and vigorous in the truth you were taught. Let your lives overflow with joy and thanksgiving for all he has done."*
> Colossians 2:7 TLB

When the river is flowing it's so easy to hear God, but in those dry seasons we often need to really push through in order to hear His voice and stay on track. God "...rewards those who earnestly seek Him"[1]. Sometimes, we need to develop our root systems; pushing and growing deep to find the pools of refreshing.

I have witnessed first-hand what happens when big trees with shallow root systems have been blown over during a storm. How many Christians have you seen come crashing down when their shallow roots in prayer and scripture have been exposed?

> *"Blessed are those whose strength is in you, whose hearts are set on pilgrimage. As they pass through the Valley of Baka,*

---

[1] Hebrews 11:6 NIV

WALKING THROUGH THE DESERT

> *they make it a place of springs;*
> *the autumn rains also cover it with pools.*
> *They go from strength to strength,*
> *till each appears before God in Zion."*
> Psalm 84:5-7 NIV

Another psalm that picks up on 'righteous paths leading to dark places', is Psalm 84. It talks about being on the '..highway to Zion, passing through the valley of tears'! What do righteous people do in the 'valley of tears'? They transform it into a spring! One of the reasons God guides us through desert times is for us to bring life to the desert. If we truly are Glory carriers, whenever we walk through the desert we will carry our living water with us to where it's most needed.

The world needs Jesus! We should be so overflowing with Him that our wells bring life to those who need it. Rather than complaining about our circumstances, how about we *change* our circumstances through tapping into the well that lives inside of us?

Why does God lead us through dark valleys? definitely so we can transform them into places of life...but also, as the psalmist says, to build up our own strength! Couch potatoes may appear to have a life of comfort that echoes the opening lines of Psalm 23, but it's in times of stretch and challenge that strength is built.

Dark Places

I want to be real with you. On occasion I have had days when the alarm clock has gone off and I've woken up in such a foul mood, I've refused to get up! At some point, my wife will get up and go about her day. Sounds of the dish washer being emptied will be accompanied by praise music drifting into the bedroom. My first reaction is one of indignation; "Who does she think she is, cheerfully singing along to those tunes...!!" But, as time drifts by, the music seems to soften my heart. Half an hour earlier I would have happily thrown my Bible across the room rather than read it; but now, as a result of the atmosphere of praise filtering through the house, my state of mind has altered, and I find myself not only opening and reading the Word of God but being pleasant to those around me!

If I'm in a dark place, I will try to lift myself out of it as much as I can manage, by putting on my worship music and reading some of the Psalms. The more I engage with the promises of God, the more I am helped. At times, I have relied solely on speaking the Lord's Prayer, repeating it many times a day, or reciting Psalm 23. If I can't bear to read, I'll listen to a podcast!

When Elijah was in a dark place and fleeing Jezebel;[1] before God spoke to him, He let Elijah sleep and provided Him food to eat. Sometimes we need our physical needs met before we are in the

---

[1] 1 Kings 19

correct state of mind to hear the voice of God. We want to give God of our best, and He is interested in our physical *and* mental health as well as our spiritual health.

Reflection

- When you have gone through hard times, has God felt close or distant?
- How have you grown through trials?

10. BUILDING BROKEN CISTERNS

"My people have committed two sins: They have forsaken me, the spring of living water, and have dug their own cisterns, broken cisterns that cannot hold water."
Jeremiah 2:13 NIV

This dire warning through Jeremiah to re-engage with the living water and build cisterns, did not say they hadn't built *any* systems, instead, it stated that they had built their *own* cisterns. The problem with many churches is that they have built their own structures based on tradition and cultural norms, rather than biblical foundations! Unfortunately, we are often blind to this.

Walk into a church and suggest a change to the service times, a change to the style of music or a change in who runs which department, and you'll often get a hugely negative reaction due to the often cultural structures in place.

Steve Miller[1] shares a story about an old Methodist church whose members religiously followed an age-old tradition when reading the Apostle's Creed; whereby they would stand up and always turn to face the back of the church! Following investigation, it was discovered that at some point in their history the church leadership had hung the creed on the balcony, as they hadn't the finances to provide books for the congregation. Some time later, enough money had finally been raised to buy the resources the church members needed, whilst the balcony had been removed during a renovation. So ingrained had this tradition become however, the congregation would still turn to face the back wall whenever they recited the Creed. Although practical and understandable at the time, this tradition was no longer a necessity and had become completely irrelevant!

Simply having structures in place does not make you a Glory carrier; you need structures that God can breathe His life into.

Stiff Necked Cisterns

Unfortunately, the people of Judah did not hold to the warning given through the prophet Jeremiah and were exiled from the promised land for seventy years. When the children of God returned; men, women and children all gathered around Ezra the High Priest, who read from the Book of the Law so that all could hear. There was loud sobbing and much wailing as Ezra read.

---

[1] The Contemporary Christian Music Debate by Steve Miller p204

Before him stood a generation of Israelites who had never heard the Law; during the years of exile it had been forgotten. So determined was this new generation not to commit the sins of their ancestors and fall back into exile, they dedicated themselves to obeying the Law of God.

Something else had been lost during the exile; the Ark of the Covenant! During the time of Jesus, the Glory of God was absent from the temple because the Ark of the Covenant had disappeared, and was no longer where God had commanded it be placed. The Holy of Holies was empty; God had left the building! Into this religious culture which did not carry the presence of God, but quickly saw the development of an all consuming obsession not to break any of His laws, the Pharisee was born.

Have you ever known a driver who, after being caught speeding, drives everywhere a few miles under the speed limit from that time on? They are so determined not to go through the ordeal of being caught for speeding again, that they drive to their own stricter speed limit, inevitably causing frustration to other road users! I believe this is what happened to the Israelites! So determined were they not to break God's laws, as the previous generation had done, they made up even stricter rules, which ensured they would always keep the laws already in existence. For example; concerning the law about not being allowed to work on the Sabbath - many more rigorous rules were set in place around it, such as dictating exactly how far you could actually walk on the Sabbath, to ensure there would be absolutely no risk of ever breaking the original law!

BUILDING BROKEN CISTERNS

The Pharisees were devout followers of God, having separated themselves from society to study and teach the Law, and from the 'common' people to keep themselves pure! They learned the first five books of the Bible off by heart and adhered not only to the written Word of God but also to the oral traditions which had been passed down through the ages. Teachers of the Law, in order to help people follow them, would bring clarifying rules and then hold these new laws to the same standard as the written Word of God! The Law had grown from 613 laws into literally the thousands! preached by religious leaders who focused on how to be spiritually pure, rather than how to help your neighbour.

Into this Culture Jesus turns up, the Word of God in the flesh, and the Pharisees don't recognise him! People who have dedicated their whole lives to The Word of God, miss The WORD of God when He turns up...and it gets worse! When Jesus performs miracles by the power of the Holy Spirit, the Pharisees accuse him of channelling evil spirits! Jesus in turn condemns the Pharisees for committing the unforgivable sin - attributing the work of the Holy Spirit to the devil! The Pharisees have dedicated themselves to building cisterns, but they themselves are cisterns that are broken and they have rejected the Holy Spirit.

One of the ways the Pharisees demonstrated their pious nature, was to walk around with their heads bowed so they wouldn't accidentally look at a woman in a lustful way. This resulted in them continually bumping their heads and causing cuts and bruises! Jesus refers to this practice when questioning them on how they can lead others into holiness when they are blind themselves; not looking where they are going!

The Pharisees were not popular with the 'ordinary' person; partly because they looked down on everyone, and partly because of the heavy burden of temple taxes and moral laws which they had pushed onto the people. Jesus said; "They (Pharisees) tie up heavy burdens and lay them on men's shoulders, but they themselves are unwilling to move with them so much as a finger."[1]

Unlike the Pharisees, Jesus was very popular! The huge crowds that constantly flocked to see him were filled with all kinds of people, ranging from the pious Pharisees to notorious sinners. However, if the Pharisees had increased the burden of the Law, then Jesus presented the Law as though pumped up on Steroids!! He would say things like; "If you are angry with someone, you are guilty of murder," or, "If you've even looked at a woman in a lustful way, you are guilty of adultery"! People were already struggling to live their lives in accordance with the Law as instructed by the Pharisees - it was tough, but just doable with enough effort; but those who listened to Jesus' teaching realised that the standard level *he* was talking about would be impossible for anyone to keep without a great deal of help, and this Jesus gave them – offering food, money and supernatural aid to those in need.

Imagine the scene; there's a huge crowd of people listening to Jesus, who have been striving every single day to live their lives

---

[1] Matthew 23:4 NASB

under the huge weight of the Law, and keep every rule, as demanded by the Pharisees. As Jesus explains that those who look at someone else lustfully are just as much a sinner in the eyes of God as an adulterer is, see the gaze of the crowd turn to focus on the cuts and bruises clearly displayed on the foreheads of the Pharisees! "Hey Pharisee!", they cry in anger and frustration, "You've been condemning us for sleeping around but you're just as bad!! Keep your eyes and your rules to yourself!"

Jesus has just told the townsfolk that the Pharisees who struggle with looking at women are just as guilty as the notorious adulterer in the crowd, and it's immediately removed a huge unnecessary burden of guilt from their shoulders! "Hypocrites! You're just as dirty!" No wonder the crowds loved Jesus, and yet the message He preached increased the standard of the Law.

When Jesus preached, lives were transformed; people were set free and healed. When the Pharisees preached, lives were put into bondage! We should never water down the biblical standard, but we also need to enable people to reach the standard we preach. This is discipleship; using the power and wisdom of God combined, to lead people into repentance through the conviction of the Holy Spirit, who will then naturally flow out and help them clean up how they live their everyday lives. Not only do we need to know our Bibles; we need to know how to use the Spiritual gifts, including Words of Wisdom, to build people up in their faith.

Modern Pharisees

Imagine one Sunday morning your pastor stands up and preaches a powerful yet vulnerable message, based on his personal struggle with lustful thoughts when seeing sexualised images of women. He shares about the wise structures he's set in place to keep himself from temptation. These include; not watching certificate 18 films, not watching television after 9pm, and not going into the local newsagent's next to the church - as he may catch a glimpse of the adult magazines prominently displayed by the counter! Such is the power and honesty of the message that many decide to follow his example and, with peer support, they stop watching tv after 9pm, stop watching certificate 18 films and avoid the local newsagent - in addition to other guidelines their pastor has given to help avoid getting caught in temptation!

A few months later, Geoff moves into the area and starts attending the church. Geoff loves Jesus and lives a morally clean life. One Sunday morning, a few friends are having a chat outside the door of the church when they see Geoff walking out of the newsagent's and back into the church building. "I don't believe it", says one, "I thought Geoff was a good guy? but to blatantly walk into that shop....!! We need to pray for his soul....his poor wife!" Then someone else pipes up; "It's worse than that! He was telling me about the United game he'd watched on Match of the Day last night. Match of the Day doesn't start 'til ten, he's watching television after 9pm!" A third person chips in; "We're going to have to watch him, we can't let him give the devil a foothold!"......

BUILDING BROKEN CISTERNS

Poor Geoff had noticed the milk was running low for the teas and coffees, so showing some initiative he'd popped out to the newsagents to buy some more! Through these actions, however, and his love of football, he had inadvertently broken the strict guidelines that a few well-intentioned people had set in place to help keep *them* from possible temptation! Geoff is now being accused of sexual immorality! He is only guilty of being servant hearted, friendly and liking football....!!

Reflection

How many times have *we* criticised someone for immorality; for breaking guidelines that were never in the Bible? In my experience, the criticisms I've heard are to do with people breaking social norms or church traditions, rather than biblical truth!

11. UNHELPFUL LAWS

As an eighteen year old lad I decided to attend Bible college for a year. Within days of starting, a class of around seventy of us – all strangers, all with differing ages - were gathered together to endure the highly embarrassing experience of the 'sex talk'! Not only were the group highly uncomfortable, our teacher was too, and the resulting 'lesson' quickly boiled down to three statements with little explanation:

1. "No guys in girls rooms, no girls in guys rooms."
2. "Don't start a romantic relationship while you are here"
   - but if you are already in a relationship and not married -
3. "Don't touch any part of someone else's body that you haven't got."

This last one wasn't very helpful for a hormone filled teenager! Firstly, my own standards meant that bottom touching was overstepping the mark outside of marriage, and yet my spiritual advisors had just appeared to have given it the green light! Secondly, I could very easily present an argument in favour of any resulting interaction between lovers, by deliberately misinterpreting the letter of this law - let me delicately point out that we all possess nipples...!!

If we aspire to the letter of the law, those who argue the law will make everything permissible; while others will make arguments to the contrary! What we need is for the law to be read *and* interpreted in the spirit that it was made.

According to the 1831 London Hackney Act, every taxi in London had to keep a bale of hay in the boot! The spirit of the law was to make sure horses were being taken care of and fed, when used as a taxi service. In 1976 it was removed from the law books, as the authorities understood the spirit of the law and had not enforced that modern taxis' – now powered by engine rather than horse - should carry hay for no apparent reason.

Canals used to be the transport network for the UK. Narrowboats moved along this network transporting goods - and often whole families cramped into the tiny living spaces! The authorities were so concerned about adults and children sharing these small spaces however, they passed a law stating there must be a partition between sleeping areas. But, as most people know, every piece of furniture like those in caravans today, are designed for maximum usage whilst taking up the minimum amount of space – so in order to show obedience to this new law, a little flap of only a few centimetres high and wide was installed to partition off the sleeping space. This flap ticked the box that the law required, as no dimensions were specified, but was completely useless as it gave no degree of separation whatsoever!

When a law is interpreted it is often filtered through a belief system. The canal boat owners believed best use of space to be more important than the protection the authorities were trying to ensure. Often, laws are implemented precisely because the natural tendency of people is to do the opposite. For a law to be truly followed in the spirit that it was written, it needs people to understand the nature and intention of the law giver.

We have a Bible that was written by the Holy Spirit, and we have the opportunity to read it through the *eyes* of the Holy Spirit. It's only with a heart and mind that have been renewed by the Spirit, however, that we can truly understand what Gods commandments mean.

> *"And do not be conformed to this world, but be transformed by the renewing of your mind, so that you may prove what the will of God is, that which is good and acceptable and perfect."*
> Romans 12:2 NASB

As a youth pastor I also had to give 'the talk'. I believe I presented a much more palatable experience than the one I'd cringed through all those years before, but I was still left with trying to negotiate that delicate balance! I know many young Christians who won't have sexual intercourse but will still engage in various substitute activities; and unless they are specifically told that these things are immoral, they will continue to practise them. However, by addressing 'said' activities in a public forum, you will always run the risk of giving other hormonally charged young folk, ideas that they would never have thought of, thereby leading them into temptation.

It's the classic dilemma of discovering that when you are told not to do something, you instantly have desires to do it!

When applying the holiness of God to our lives, we need to remember that our words and actions, without love at the centre, are no more than a hideous racket that will drive people away from God.

Reflection
- Where have you seen 'laws' deliberately misinterpreted to allow people the freedoms they desire?
- Have you experienced a 'law' that was designed for good but used for evil?

12. BE FLEXIBLE

One of the first healings I witnessed was that of a lady who'd been injured in a car accident; resulting brain damage meant she now had trouble speaking and so her friend had brought her to the ministry time. As I prayed for this woman to be healed of brain damage, she immediately started talking to me about a darkness that had lived inside of her since the accident! I asked if she had accepted Jesus into her life, and when she replied "Yes!", I attempted to teach her that the demonic had no power over her and darkness could not be living on the inside! This lady was absolutely adamant I was wrong, insisting repeatedly that darkness did live inside of her and so in the end - just to shut her up really - I agreed to pray!

So how do you prayer when you don't know what to do? I did the logical thing; put my hands gently round her face and began to pray in tongues. Immediately, her face contorted and her bones started cracking and popping! I stopped praying and asked if she was okay? She replied that something was happening and to carry on! So, I continued to pray in tongues and this lady's face was flexing and making sounds that I had never heard before, and then I saw this black thing suddenly peel away from her face and fly off to the side! Immediately her face stopped contorting, she opened her eyes and said, "It's gone!"

Although I'm obviously happy about this, I am also very conflicted! I have three problems; the first, is that according to the scriptures I have read, I do not believe the enemy can live in a Christian! Secondly, I had been taught through scripture that tongues are a prayer to God and useless in spiritual warfare. The third, was the fact that this lady received her injuries through a car accident and not from some curse or other demonic activity!

My Bible based doctrines have just been smashed into a wall of experience! Jesus says to the apostle Philip; "If you don't believe the words I say to you, believe in my works..."[1] In other words; "Philip, believe, because of what you have experienced!" Our experience should challenge our thinking. Our experience should challenge our doctrine.

I don't believe we should define our beliefs based purely on our experience, that would be a dangerous road to go down, but our experience should challenge our doctrine! The Bible is infallible but my understanding is not!

I have since learned that tongues are a great weapon in spiritual warfare and that the devil will often get in through trauma! Many Christians have the influence of the enemy upon their lives; call it

---

[1] John 14:11

a stronghold! I'm not sure how to explain it but the spiritual dimension affects us more than we realise.

How did this experience change me? I decided to treat all sickness as if it was a demon. The result? more healings! Please note; I am *not* saying that everyone who has a sickness has a demon!!

I think we need to be humble enough to admit that we do not know it all. We need to read our Bibles and we need to study theology. We should also know that God is bigger than our own understanding!

Reflection
Have you held doctrinal beliefs that your experience or study has convinced you were in error, or incomplete? How fervently did you once hold to those beliefs? What current doctrinal issues are being challenged?

13. BUILDING BLOCKS OF LIFE

When I teach about being a Glory Carrier, sooner or later people will always ask me; "But what are the structures that are needed to contain His Glory?" They are no great secret! The issue is, that as we grow into more maturity we still search for that secret, hidden truth that our heroes of the faith must have found, and yet, all the legends I know of talk about the fundamental building blocks as being things we already know:

- Pray
- Access the Bible
- Listen to the voice of God
- Meditate on what God has said.
- Live a life of biblical morality
- Create accountable relationships (James 5:16)
- Remain connected to the church body
- Submit your finances to God
- Sabbath rest
- Whatever God says, do it!

Let's delve a little deeper into the first two on the list.

A Life of Prayer

"You do not have because you do not ask God."
James 4:2 NIV

It's amazing how many people when faced with a crisis, will first call their pastor before taking time to give it to the Lord in prayer. Jesus would often find a place of solitude and spend time speaking with His Father. If Jesus found the need to build a foundation of prayer into His life, how much more should we turn to prayer!

Prayer is an issue that most Christians struggle with. Ask any Christian if they need to pray more and even those who devote hours of their day to prayer will probably answer; "Yes"!

Marathon not a Sprint

"...let us run with endurance the race that is set before us."
Hebrews 12:1 NASB

We've all been there; after hearing an inspiring story of how someone's life has radically changed following a forty day fast, and having never fasted for more than a day ourselves, we decide to emulate the story, only to get disappointed with ourselves when three days in we find ourselves chomping on a naughty chocolate bar! Or, we hear the testimony of an incredible hero of the faith who attributes their spiritual power and energy to a three hour prayer time every morning. Next day, our alarm goes off at 3am! Ten minutes later we've run out of words.....by the end of the third day we've either given up completely, or become so irritable that we're snapping at anyone who even looks at us the wrong way!!!

If God tells you to do something, then do it, no matter how strange or illogical it may seem! Most of the time though, I find God just gives me a gentle nudge in the right direction – encouraging me to pray more, for example. If you've never had a prayer time before, start with a target of ten minutes. If you end up praying for an hour, awesome! but don't get disheartened if you barely manage ten minutes – see it as success! You hit your target! If you manage ten minutes, then why not try and increase it to twenty minutes!

If you feel the nudge to fast, my advice would be to only fast for a single day for the first few times, before progressing to two or three days! In other words; if you are working on Godly principles, lay your foundations brick by brick by setting realistic goals. If on the other hand God tells you to do something specific, then go and do that.

What does it mean to pray for three hours?

When I say I spent the morning in prayer, that doesn't mean I spent three hours asking God for things, far from it! In fact, if I spend thirty minutes in prayer probably most of it would *not* have been me asking for things. Have you noticed that the Lord's Prayer can be said in under a minute? The most common word for prayer in the New Testament is 'proseuchē' and can be translated as 'an exchange of wishes'! When we come to prayer, we come into the

Presence of the Father and lay our wishes or desires before Him, and in exchange we pick up His desires.

> *"Prayer does not change God, but it*
> *changes those who pray."*
> Soren Kierkegaard

Rightly or wrongly, for me, the word 'prayer' is interchangeable with the phrase; 'Seeking God.' When I have a time of prayer, some may call it a devotional time, my aim is to encounter God; to learn about Him. The Apostle Paul teaches us that we can gaze into the face of God as we do a mirror, and as we do, we are transformed into His likeness.[1]

Prayer can definitely include having a whinge and asking for needs to be met, but there is so much more! Prayer allows us to soar above our problems and view the world from a heavenly perspective. Prayer is a two-way conversation! God loves to speak with us, and we find ourselves being transformed as we spend time in His Presence. Prayer is about having your whole being renewed with eternal life. Prayer is about having our desires and outlook aligned with Heaven.

When we pray the Lord's Prayer, we pray that God's Will, His desires, will come to pass on the Earth. Genesis teaches us that we

---

[1] 2 Cor 3:18

were literally made from the earth, so a great place to start is to ask for God's Will to be manifested in our bodies.

One morning I was in prayer and bringing an issue to Father. I was in conflict with another leader, we were literally at logger heads, and virtually everything I said seemed to be taken as an insult or misinterpreted! It felt like this leader was deliberately attacking me and I was at my wits end! With a final plea I handed it over to God; and as I hung on to Him in utter desperation, Father gave me a picture in my mind of this leader who was also in deep prayer on the other side of town! He was crying out to God; "Why is Chris attacking me, why is he persecuting me?!" My immediate response was to pray blessing upon that leader, success in their ministry and favour in their family. As a result of that prayer the issue between me and that leader was instantly resolved. What had happened? I had gone to God, given Him my wishes and then been given a perspective from Heaven, which led me to pray God's Will upon my colleague rather than my own!

It's All About Heart!

I prefer my personal prayer to my public prayer as I can be really honest! I don't get tied up in being theologically correct or making sure I'm using the correct form of prayer; instead, I can bare my heart and say what I really think without restraint. The veil has been lifted and I can go right into my Heavenly Fathers court and make my case before His throne. I can be real, honest and heart felt.

GLORY CARRIERS

"During the days of Jesus' life on earth, he offered up prayers and petitions with fervent cries and tears to the one who could save him from death, and he was heard because of his reverent submission."
Hebrews 5:7 NIV

I remember when we first put our daughter into the local playgroup. We'd invited many of the children to her birthday party at a local soft play, but unfortunately only a couple of the parents had replied. It may seem like a small thing but I was quite distressed! I couldn't bear the thought of my daughter feeling rejected having only a couple of children at her party. I called out to God! It wasn't really words, more of a cry of anguish that came from deep inside of me out to my Father. Next day the replies came flooding back accepting the party invitation!

God always knows what you mean, even when you struggle to put it into words! He knows your heart! Don't put on a mask; be real, be reckless, throw yourself on Him and let Him utterly amaze you. I believe authenticity in prayer trumps technique.

Dig into the Word

"All Scripture is inspired by God and is useful to teach us what is true and to make us realize what is wrong in our lives. It corrects us when we are wrong and teaches us to do what is right."
2 Timothy 3:16 NLT

As I've already said, the most common way for me to hear God speaking is through my Bible. When I open my Bible I mostly know where I'm going to turn, either because I feel led to a certain passage, or because I want to delve deeper into some verses that have piqued my interest.

Although I often feel the urge to throw off all restraint on directed Bible reading, I've realised that this approach does not build a sound biblical foundation in my life! I don't use Bible notes as they're not particularly helpful to me, and although I've attempted a study which completes the whole Bible in a year through breaking it down into daily bitesize chunks, I found it frustrating! I often wanted to continue reading a particular passage, or would miss a few days and then get disheartened.

What does work for me, is a structured reading plan which completes the Bible in a year but gives me the freedom to read as much or as little as I like in one go! Printed on a single piece of A4 paper, I simply tick off chapters as I complete them. A quick search on the internet will reveal many of these plans for free. They allow me to delve into a certain book and do a weeks worth of reading in a day, but similarly, allow me to miss a week if I have other studies and come back without any feelings of guilt or disappointment. Although the weeks are marked out, I can ignore them and work through the passages in the order that is most helpful to me!

I recommend finding some type of plan which will help you read through the entire Bible; whether it takes three months or three years is irrelevant, it's all about what works for you! If Bible notes are useful to you, invest in them! If the 'Bible in a year' is most helpful, go for it! If reading right through from Genesis to Revelation is best for you – do it! We live in a privileged age with access to multiple editions of the Bible. I have many different versions filling my bookshelf and downloaded to my phone. One way to begin reading is to buy a new translation!

One of the things I find people coming to talk to me most often about, after I've preached on reading the Bible, is their struggle with literacy. I realise that when someone who struggles with reading is told that they need to read the Bible, which let's be honest, in most translations is not the easiest book to read; they can find it really daunting! It's important that we don't make literacy a pre-requisite for the kingdom! There are currently many apps that will read the Bible to you on your smart phone and create interactive Bible studies. If you don't possess a smart phone, the Bible in the format of a CD is readily available.

Although I fully support reading the Bible over listening to a preached word or reading Christian books etc; I do think it's very easy to become too much of a purist! We live in a multi-media world competing for our attention. For many people, reading a book is a habit sadly lost apart from the occasional novel. I fill my life with podcasts, praise music and teaching videos. There are times we should shun technology in the day to day, and I often wish we could go back to a simpler less connected world. However, as we look to disciple ourselves and others, I don't believe we should let the written word become an unnecessary barrier – the primary connection should always be between God and ourselves; not education or culture.

I've already mentioned that the primary way God speaks to me is through reading my Bible; the second, is through listening to someone preaching via podcast, however, time after time I'll tune into one of my favourite speakers before inevitably turning the message off half-way through, realising that I've long since disappeared down a huge rabbit warren in my mind, chasing thoughts with the Holy Spirit, and haven't got a clue what the preacher's talking about! It's as though hearing someone else share the Word of God activates the voice of God inside of me! The third way I hear God speak is through listening to Praise music.

Reflection
Other ways I hear God speak? - through creation, in my dreams, through my friends, being a son, a husband and a father. What helps you connect with God?

14. VEHICLES OF GLORY

God's promise to his chosen people is that He is a God who is present. Right from the Garden of Eden, He wanted to walk with us and be with us. In the Old Covenant, this was represented by the Ark of the Covenant which the manifest presence of God would appear upon. Wherever the children of God travelled, they carried the Ark with them. It's a beautiful representation of God going on the journey with us, keeping us in step with Him.

During the reign of King David the Ark had been captured by the Philistines, who later abandoned it because of the disaster it was causing their nation. In second Samuel, David sets off to retrieve the Ark of the Covenant. It's such an important occasion that he takes thirty thousand specially chosen men with him, plus anyone else he can gather to join them on this momentous adventure! They decide to put the Ark on a cart to transport it back to Jerusalem. However, not just any cart will do! Out of honour and deference to such an important and precious cargo, it has to be a new cart!

VEHICLES OF GLORY

Imagine the scene; over thirty thousand people marching out together, playing every instrument they could lay their hands on and singing as one voice in exuberant, excited celebration! It would have been deafeningly loud and the greatest honour they could show. Why? Because God was coming home to live amongst His people again!

Then disaster strikes! The oxen stumble, and to prevent the Ark falling from the cart, a man called Uzzah puts out his hand to steady it, and he physically touches the Ark! God's anger burns against Uzzah for displaying such a lack of reverence and He strikes him dead on the spot! You can imagine the festivities suddenly coming to an abrupt halt and an uncomfortable hush falling upon the crowd!

When I read passages like this, I do ask myself the question; "Do I know this God?" It seems so unfair to me, and I cannot find any satisfactory explanation that could possibly bring any comfort or understanding to the family and friends of poor Uzzah! But I do know this; the Glory of God was never meant to be carried on the vehicles and structures of man. The heavy manifest Glory of God was always meant to be carried on the shoulders of His priests.

We, as God's chosen people, are His Glory carriers. It's not about the songs, the books or the style; the Glory of God was designed to rest on His people. Denominations, styles of service, preaching and ministry are just our eulogy; some are better than others for enabling people to connect with God, but it's always been about people, not structures.

When we use the vehicles of man to ram-raid God's presence into a situation - people get hurt, people lose their faith, people die...

I am not saying there isn't an 'anointing' on a certain song, but the heavy Glory of God has always been designed to dwell on, and in, people. What happens when you tire of that song? What happens if you are imprisoned and denied access to a Bible, church service or preacher? We have tools to help us engage with the Presence of God, but my Bible says that nothing can separate me from His love; from Him. Do not rely on a crutch, rely on God himself.

When ministers ask for advice on releasing the presence of God within their church, they often ask the wrong questions. Usually, they're looking for set structures and plans which can be installed and implemented, but the secret is much more simple; His presence rests on hungry hearts! Structures and procedures are there to build and disciple people - they're all about the people. A hungry heart is all about God!

While reading this story in second Samuel, I found my interest drawn to the reaction of King David, when the mishandling of the Ark containing the Glory of God resulted in the death of Uzzah. David says; "How can I bring the Ark home?" In other words; "How can I handle this Glory?", "How can I control it...?" David was unwilling to continue moving the Ark into the city, so took it aside to rest in the house of a man called Obed-Edom. King David, *the* go-to biblical character to learn about worship ministry; to learn about encountering the presence of God - this same man who had a heart after God's own heart; and when playing his harp, would cause the room to be flooded with such a sweet presence of God that devils would have to flee! This very same David abandons the manifest presence of God; abandons God living amongst his people!

Abandoning the Presence

After the death of Uzzah, it takes three months before David is willing to go back and encounter the formidable Ark of the Covenant again! In that time, we learn that Uzzah's family have been greatly blessed by God; but also, when the Philistines later attack, David defeats them after spending time enquiring of the Lord. Far from being punished, God seems to be blessing David and the Bible says that during this period "...the fame of David went out into all the lands; and the Lord brought the fear of him (David) on all the nations."

David hasn't abandoned God! He's still praying to Him, still living for Him; but he *has* built a barrier between himself and the 'terrifying', manifest presence of God. This has been done to provide some measure of protection for him and his people, and to maintain some semblance of control. Yet in that period, David *still* experiences the favour of God! I can almost imagine him thinking; *"I want God, but I don't want to be that close to God; face to face with Him in His Glory. That intimacy is frightening, that intimacy can kill!"*

When I say this, I immediately see a parallel between Word and Spirit churches in this nation. There are kings and church leaders who have seen the misuse of the spiritual gifts and power of God, directed against the people of God. They have witnessed division, pain and people turning away in droves as the anointing of God has been misused; but some have gone on to build amazing, large and influential churches that impact regions and local authorities. They have gained favour with councils and established organisations through their inclusive programmes and social action work. Many unchurched people have re-engaged with church because of their ministry, and as a result have found Jesus. These churches are dripping in the blessing of God, and yet, their ministry is focused around programmes and teaching rather than the manifest heavy presence of God being in their midst!

There are also churches like the household of Obed-Edom. These Spirit churches have the presence of God at the centre of all they do. In everything, they are blessed by God and usually successful. Stories get passed around about how amazing it is to be part of their house. However, they remain small; not transforming a city or growing in favour with the authorities in the region. Everything they do is good and yet, in the most part, irrelevant to saving a nation. There is no vision or structural outworking to affect the region other than in a haphazard and local way.

I was warmly pondering this theoretical thought as a passenger in a car one morning, and thinking about how it applied to churches I personally knew, when I felt the Holy Spirit speak to me with the words of the prophet Nathan; "That man is you!" This immediately cut across my thought pattern bringing conviction to my heart. I instantly realised that through the use of much logical reasoning and circumstance, I too had erected barriers to protect myself from the manifest, intimate presence of God, just as David had!

I knew that in the last four years I had grown in stature. I had more influence, more blessing, more favour with people, and was more gifted and practiced in the use of ministry gifts and running a church. However, I was not as hungry for the presence of God as I had been four years earlier. I was not so abandoned to the intimacy of the Holy Spirit as I once was.

We often sing songs that talk about desiring God; that we are 'thirsty' for Him! My question is; "How thirsty are you?" Have you learned to live a form of Christianity that doesn't need God to do the impossible because you have already worked out all the possibilities? Have you settled for the level of spiritual experience you're currently at because you know that to go deeper will cost you?

Part of Jesus being Lord is that He is in control. We need to learn to love the river not just a stream; to be in that place where our feet can't touch the floor and the current is pushing us towards our destiny!

Once we believe that the Holy Spirit is poured out so we can experience better worship services, I believe we are swimming against the flow. Jesus said He would send us the Holy Spirit so that we would be a witness - the river of God flows towards the dead sea! I am not an evangelist but I *have* found that the gifts of healing and prophecy are more powerful with the lost than in the church!

I don't know about you, but I believe it's time for me to get back into the river and allow God's current to take me wherever He wants. It may be frightening on occasion; I may sometimes feel like I'm about to drown - and I know my behaviour may definitely be a little out of control at times, but either God is Lord of my life or He's not!

The living water had been poured out upon our church family, however, we were a broken cistern that couldn't contain it! And yet, though we are *all* broken clay pots – broken containers of the Glory of God - He is still willing to continually pour out His Glory through our brokenness! So, no matter the pain and hurt I may be experiencing, and though I may feel far from ready, I choose to look to the heavens and cry; "Come Lord Jesus....Let it RAIN....."

ABOUT THE AUTHOR

Christopher Fleetcroft is part of the leadership team at Revive Church, Hull, UK. Part of the Revive Network team; a movement of churches and leaders dedicated to building and planting growing, powerful, presence-filled 21st century churches, Christopher minsters across the UK and beyond.

Christopher and his wife, Lesley, have been married for thirteen years, and live in the East Riding of Yorkshire.

For further information and contact details please visit
www.glorycarriers.co.uk

Printed in Great Britain
by Amazon

41510101R00058